OFFICE FOR STA
IN EDUCAT

First Class

The Standards and Quality of Education in Reception Classes

A report from the Office of
Her Majesty's Chief Inspector of Schools

London : HMSO

Office for Standards in Education
Elizabeth House
York Road
London SE1 7PH

Tel: 071-925 6800

ISBN 0 11 350020 3

CONTENTS

INTRODUCTION

In the autumn term 1992 HMI visited 88 English primary schools to inspect the work in 141 reception classes. The schools were located in 41 local education authorities (LEAs) and were selected to represent different types of locality. About half the schools served areas with significant to severe degrees of social and economic disadvantage.

The purposes of the inspections were to assess the standards of work and quality of provision in reception classes (Year R), and to appraise the effectiveness of the arrangements for admission and for enlisting parents in helping the children to make a good start at school.

- Despite variations in the social and economic backgrounds of the children the overall standards of work were satisfactory or better in nearly 80 per cent of the reception classes.

- The ages at which the children entered the reception classes ranged from just four years to five years and three months. This meant that some children received over three terms more primary education than others depending upon the admission arrangements of the school.

- About 90 per cent of the children had attended some form of pre-school provision. Most of the schools had links with the main playgroups, nursery classes and nursery schools which the children had attended but the level and quality of this contact differed considerably.

- All the schools valued partnership with the children's parents but there were considerable differences in the ways in which this was promoted.

- In very many schools the teaching of children in reception classes is benefiting from the clearer targets provided by the National Curriculum for older infant children.

- All the reception classes gave a high priority to teaching the early stages of literacy and, to a lesser extent, numeracy. In very many schools, but not all, the pupils were given a sound start in learning to read and write.

- Standards of behaviour and the quality of relationships between the children, and between the adults and the children in the reception classes, were almost always good.

The vast majority of the children settled in quickly to their first class.

- Most of the schools invested considerable time and effort in assessing the children. Few involved parents in the initial assessment of the children and many did not exploit the information gained from assessment to inform curriculum planning.

- There was considerable variation in the accommodation and, to a lesser extent, resourcing of reception classes. Levels of staffing varied markedly with adult to child ratios ranging from 6:1 to 35:1. In those reception classes with a well qualified teacher and a suitably qualified assistant standards were usually better.

1.   Statutory education in England begins in the term after a child's fifth birthday. At this age children are required to follow the National Curriculum and the programmes of study set down for Key Stage 1.

2.   In practice most children are admitted to school between their fourth and fifth birthdays. In the schools inspected 57 per cent of children entered their first class as reception pupils (YR) between four and four and a half years old. The remaining 43 per cent began school some months before or after their fifth birthday. Thus for the majority of the reception class pupils the National Curriculum was not legally applicable until up to a year after they began school.

3.   Although pre-school provision of education is discretionary and has developed in different ways across the country nearly all the children in this survey had attended some form of pre-school provision before starting school. Over 57 per cent had atended playgroup or private nursery provision, about 34 per cent had attended a LEA nursery class and less than 10 per cent a LEA nursery school.

The transition from home to school

4.   The inspections took place early in the autumn term. It was clear that the children entered school not only at different ages but with widely different educational experience gained from the opportunities offered in their home, community and pre-school. That wide mix of pre-school experience posed considerable challenges for the reception teachers in providing a smooth transition from home to school and in providing teaching which matched the range of development of the children. Unsurprisingly, all the schools deemed it necessary to find out as much as possible about the children they were admitting.

5. Most of the schools liaised with the pre-school providers. Much liaison was informal and helped to build a good relationship with the child. Links with nursery provision, where it existed, varied in quality and links with playgroups were even more tenuous. There were good examples of close co-operation, but there were also cases where the school had little contact, and failed to exploit these important sources of information about individual children. Occasionally playgroups were asked to contribute to initial assessments. Where a nursery class was linked to a primary school the assessment process was nearly always thorough and was often part of the school's assessement and recording procedures.

6. Almost all the schools carried out an early assessment of the pupils in order to determine their starting points for learning. In around one in ten schools a teacher visited the child at home and with the parent completed an entry assessment. A further 37 per cent of schools assessed the pupils in the first term in school while over half the schools used a combination of initial and continuous assessment. Although there were regular consultations between parents and teachers, very few schools asked parents to contribute to their child's assessment. Despite the amount of time devoted to detailed assessment it was rare for schools to plan the work based on pupils' levels of achievement at entry. It was more usual for assessment to be used as a form of 'screening' to identify pupils with learning difficulties and special educational needs.

7. The arrangements for familiarising pupils and parents with the school's provision for the reception class varied considerably in the number of pre-visits and the patterns of pupils' entry to school. Generally schools tried to keep parents informed and to build good relationships with them.

8. Many of the schools took steps to help parents understand the content of the curriculum and the teaching methods used, thus assisting them to see how they might contribute to their

children's progress at home and complement the work of the school.

9.   In those few cases where induction arrangements were poor, it was sometimes because the pupils began school, full-time, too abruptly with little opportunity to visit beforehand or for a short period of part-time attendance. However, some schools that had improved their induction procedures to provide for a smooth entry to the reception class, initially encountered some opposition from governors and from parents who believed the children were put at a disadvantage if they were not given full-time places as soon as possible. Such opposition was not usually sustained. When more gradual induction became the norm this was widely accepted as beneficial.

10.   A few successful schools were as flexible as the circumstances allowed in their arrangements for entry to the reception class. They focused upon accommodating to the needs of the child and the parents rather than applying hard and fast rules. Thus if a child clearly signalled he or she was capable of benefiting from full-time attendance from the start, provision was made accordingly. On the other hand, parents of children for whom part-time attendance was judged preferable were offered that option.

11.   The quality of work in about 80 per cent of the reception classes was satisfactory or better. This is a better match of work to pupils' ability than is generally the case in primary classes. The pupils' social development was effectively fostered and they were provided with sound and intellectually challenging teaching related to the first levels of the subjects of the NC. Over 84 per cent of the schools were successful in teaching the early stages of literacy. Where the work was effective the important aspects of literacy – reading, writing, speaking and listening – were carefully planned and incorporated into the whole curriculum as well as the target for some direct teaching, for example, of reading skills. Teachers used a balanced range of teaching methods. There were opportunities for pupils to write about their activities and commonly there was also systematic teaching of letter shapes, letter sounds, letter patterns, frequently occurring words and handwriting. These approaches were usually appropriately timed and provided a suitable preparation for the early stages of English in the National Curriculum.

12.   Valuable early literacy activities were evident in the vast majority of the classes. For example, the children enjoyed attractive and suitable books. They used information, library and picture books and were generally introduced appropriately to reading with books that were carefully chosen and graded by difficulty often as the introductory stage of a published reading scheme. Practically all the schools operated home/school reading programmes involving parents. Most teachers were adept at using stories and reading good quality literature which captured the children's interests and fired their imagination. Some excellent story sessions involving the whole class were witnessed where the enrichment and extension of the children's vocabulary and use of English were clearly evident.

13.   The pupils made less progress in reading and writing in those classes where there was a poorly planned programme and

limited teaching strategies. Often in such classes there was a premature use and over-dependence on worksheets which impoverished the pupils' experience of language.

14.   In contrast to the emphasis given to introducing reading and writing, speaking and listening were not emphasised enough in about half of the schools. Better overall standards in literacy were achieved where the development of spoken English was taken seriously and well planned. When this occurred, there was regular story-telling, class and group discussion and effective questioning; adults took time to talk with the pupils; drama and role play were used effectively and the teacher's or other adult's spoken language was a good model for the children. All these features helped the pupils to increase their stock of words, use them flexibly according to purpose and develop their competence in using English.

15.   About three-quarters of the classes established good foundations for understanding number. The main gains occurred where the teachers introduced mathematical language through a wide range of number activities. In these classrooms the pupils had good reasons to sort, estimate, count and calculate. A core structure for the work was often provided by a commercial scheme amply extended by well planned practical work. Unsuitably used, the schemes resulted in poor work such as colouring in prescribed shapes and pictures and, when combined with lack of discussion, resulted in little worthwhile learning.

16.   Rarely were schools able to make good provision for outdoor play. Very few had self-contained areas for outdoor play or immediate, easy access to play space appropriate for young children. Consequently the pupils' developing physical abilities including gross motor skills, strength and stamina were often catered for in only limited ways through indoor physical education lessons. In addition lack of space sometimes meant that access was restricted to other valuable learning activities for example with sand and water.

17.   In general the teaching techniques used in the reception classes were quite flexible. It was common for the teacher to draw the whole class together for an introductory session followed by focused teaching of each of several groups while keeping a watchful eye on them all.

18.   There was a clear connection between good standards overall and the use of a mix of teaching techniques. Over 75 per cent of the teachers used a range of teaching techniques competently including instruction, exposition, demonstration, questioning and listening. They intervened appropriately to sustain and extend activities, used well-timed questioning to refine what the pupils were doing and thinking, built on their interests and experiences, explained processes carefully and clarified instructions. The valuable element, often missing in otherwise good work, was that of drawing pupils together after a session of related group activities to consolidate what had been learnt through discussion and direct teaching.

19.   In the fifth or so of classes with less satisfactory teaching there was a cluster of common weaknesses. These included too much time spent on basic class management such as lining up; inappropriate use of whole class sessions for control, not teaching; a lack of adult involvement in the children's learning; and the adoption of a supervisory rather than a teaching role.

20.   Two-thirds of the teachers organised their classes so that for some of the time small groups of between four and six pupils worked on different activities at the same time. Sometimes the activities related to one subject – most frequently English or mathematics – but usually more than two subjects were involved. The success of this mixed-activity approach depended upon the degree of coherence acheived between the activities rather than the number of activities on offer. Sometimes coherence was achieved by a unifying theme or topic, such as 'growing things', or by a common experience, such as a walk or visit.

21.   The organisational strategies and the teaching techniques were affected by the number of pupils and the number of adults in each class. Roughly a third of classes had between 20–25 pupils, a third between 26–30 and a third between 31–35. However, the inspections took place in the autumn term when many classes were not yet complete. In 32 per cent of lessons there was only one adult – the teacher; in 45 per cent two adults and in 21 per cent three or more. The child/adult ratios varied from 6:1 to 35:1. Standards were usually better in the classes with two adults and only reception-aged pupils.

22.   Non-teaching assistance made an important contribution to standards and quality. This was invariably better where the assistant had a suitable qualification. Of considerable significance was the quality of the adults' relationships and interaction with the pupils. When the lessons were at their best, the adults provided clearly established codes of behaviour, models of clear expression and the ability to sustain and extend talk and play.

23.   In the most successful classes, while the teachers were adaptable and moved effectively between concentrating on a group to a more general supporting role, the other adults had a more restricted role. Most remained with either one or two set groups or worked with individual pupils.

24.   The best lessons achieved a good balance between teacher direction and the pupil's selection of activities. Importantly, where there was choice the teacher noted how the pupils used their time and what activities they chose to ensure no-one wasted time or spent too much time on particular activities.

25.   The quality of learning through play presented rather a dismal picture. Fewer than half of the teachers fully exploited the educational potential of play. In more than a third of the

schools play was only recreational; it lacked an educational purpose and was usually undertaken only after work had been completed. It was largely ignored by adults but sometimes regarded as a useful time filler when pupils were tiring of the main work. In the poorer classes teachers over-directed work and under-directed play. They used play as a reward for finishing work or as an occupational or holding device. By contrast, in the effective classes play was used positively to develop children's abilities across a wide range of activities. For example, the provision of 'home corners', sand and water play activities which are long-standing features of the work with young children were planned into the programme with a sound educational purpose rather than as time fillers.

26. Four out of five of the schools inspected provided a suitably broad programme for pupils in the reception class which effectively introduced aspects of all the subjects in the National Curriculum. Within a quarter of the schools, however, there was sometimes an over-emphasis on sedentary tasks. Where this occurred, insufficient time was left for practical activity or exploratory play with equipment or materials. In about a quarter, too, there was an under-emphasis of some parts of the curriculum, particularly science and technology.

27. In the fifth of the schools which did not provide a satisfactory curriculum for reception pupils the main weakness was a significant lack of demand associated with under-expectation of the children. The work was often narrow and shallow; activities lacked purpose and were mainly occupational.

28. The development of reading, writing and number skills received high priority in the majority of the schools. About 10 per cent of schools dealt with either literacy or number work in a narrow and over-prescriptive way. Often this was caused by an inappropriate concentration and over-use of published schemes, workbooks and heavily-directed pencil and paper exercises, usually at the expense of language enrichment and good quality art, music, science and technology.

29. Schools were at very different stages in developing or updating their curriculum guidelines and few made explicit reference to provision in the reception class. A few referred to the learning needs of young pupils, the importance of firsthand experiences and building on what children had learned at home.

Planning the curriculum

30. As a method of long-term planning more than three-quarters of the teachers linked together the many parts of

the curriculum under common themes or topics. In most cases, these formed part of a whole-school programme for topic work which was taught on a two, three, or four-yearly cycle. In the majority of the schools, topics tended to last half a term, but more than 10 per cent of schools expected them to last a whole term.

31. Longer-term planning frequently included flow diagrams showing how different activities and subjects related to the topic. Short-term planning broke down the work into activities, usually for a week or fortnight. Seven out of ten schools related the skills and competencies to be taught to the National Curriculum. Just over half of these referred to the National Curriculum Attainment Targets, the Statements of Attainment and Levels of Achievement while the remainder also referred to the Programmes of Study.

32. The quality of planning was very mixed. At best there was an excellent framework for sequencing the work and indicating how it would be taught and managed. The themes or topics were analysed by subjects into related activities and key learning objectives which were assessed, for example under 'children are able to . . . ' headings. In these schools, curricular planning had a clear rationale that linked reception class provision to the National Curriculum without unduly forcing subject divisions while recognising that some focused teaching of subjects was necessary.

33. Very few School Development Plans made explicit reference to reception-aged pupils. Where the plan recognised the needs of these pupils it usually had a good effect, for example schools were not overly influenced by National Curriculum requirements but kept them in mind when planning work.

Impact of the National Curriculum on provision in reception classes

34. Less than 10 per cent of reception class teachers felt unduly pressurised by the school and/or parents to meet the requirements of the National Curriculum. Where there was such pressure teachers related it directly to the assessment at age seven by the Standard Assessment Tasks (SATs) and to giving the children 'a good start'.

35. Other reception class teachers recognised the need to keep the National Curriculum in mind when planning. They took account of play and experimental learning and were careful to introduce the more formal elements of the National Curriculum in accordance with the pupils' developing abilities. Most teachers reported that they found the statutory orders and aspects of the non-staturory guidance a valuable backcloth for their work.

36. In only a few schools did the reception class teachers express difficulty about finding enough time to teach and assess important aspects of the work such as literacy and numeracy. These teachers generally felt that the whole curriculum or some subjects such as science were too broad. On the other hand some schools emphasised that the National Curriculum had broadened or enhanced their approach to the curriculum of the reception class and had helped them to set clearer goals and curricular objectives.

37.   It was noticeable that the commitment of the headteacher to the education of young children played a critical part in the development of good quality provision for pupils in the reception class. Experience of teaching this age group on the part of the headteacher was not necessarily associated with high quality provision: there were examples of headteachers whose teaching background was with older pupils but who were nevertheless well informed, aware of the importance of early years education and deployed resources and the expertise of their staff effectively. Difficulties arose when the head undervalued the work of the reception classes and did not appreciate the demands upon teachers. Problems also arose in schools where staff turnover affecting reception classes was high leading to discontinuity of curricular provision. In a few of the primary schools oversight of the reception class was the responsibility of a co-ordinator or the deputy head. In the best circumstances this afforded a status to the reception class which helped to realise the potential of early years' work. This suggests that bringing the reception class within the remit of a senior management post increases the possibility for success.

38.   Heads pointed out that the Local Management of Schools (LMS) had made them and the staff more cost-conscious. In many cases LMS had enabled improvements to be made to reception class provision. In a few schools, however, financial problems had led to budget deficits resulting in larger classes and staffing difficulties.

39.   In the past, HMI inspection of reception classes has often reported considerable weaknesses in the work with under-fives. It is very encouraging, therefore, to report that the findings of this survey show that about 80 per cent of what was seen was satisfactory or better and the best work of the reception classes was very good indeed. The crucial importance of getting things right in the children's first class, not only for meeting their immediate educational needs but also for establishing a sound foundation from which to progress, for example, towards work on the early stages of the National Curriculum was clearly recognised in the majority of the schools. The advent of the National Curriculum has thrown many issues concerning provision for the reception class into sharp relief, often forcing schools to address the educational needs of this age group more urgently and intensively than ever before.

40.   Teachers of reception classes have to ensure that the children make an effective transition from home to full-time primary education. Enlisting the help of parents is a key feature of effective transition. In the best circumstances the schools inspire parents to support the educational progress of their children at home and at school. In such schools the reception class teacher often becomes an important educational ambassador to parents: a role which involves much more than simply transmitting useful information about such matters as admission arrangements and school routines.

41.   It is an obvious but important point that the high degree of dependency of young children on their parents and teachers provides a common cause to which even the most disadvantaged parents can relate. The simple fact that many parents have to bring their children to and from school means that the opportunities for contact and communication with the school are probably greater than most parents will experience at any other time. Effective schools recognise the potential this has for

putting their relationships with parents on a firm footing and winning their co-operation in the best interests of the education of their children.

42. How high-quality reception class provision is achieved will depend very largely on the school's existing circumstances. Nevertheless, there are some general principles based on the findings of this report which it may be helpful for governors, heads and teachers to consider. High-quality provision and good standards of work are associated with:

- the recruitment of staff, well-qualified by training and/or experience for work with reception class pupils: professional support which fully recognises the complex and demanding task of providing a suitable curriculum for the age group which dovetails successfully into the National Curriculum;

- enlisting the help of parents with a focus upon involving them in supporting their children's learning;

- the length of time children spend in the reception class. This suggests that wherever possible three terms in the reception classes, i.e. early entry, is to be preferred. This is particularly important for summer-born children who as a group are most likely to have the shortest time in the reception class and in primary school. They need, however, a pattern of admission suited to their needs;

- the provision of a broad and balanced programme for the reception year and attention paid to planning the curriculum for the reception class at all levels – classteacher, year group and whole school;

- priority given to teaching the skills of literacy and numeracy. This is not to say that the most effective schools focus narrowly on these aspects of the work; rather that they provide a rich and varied but manageable programme of work which secures ample opportunities for pupils to listen carefully to good models of language, speak clearly and confidently, increase and use their vocabulary imaginatively, and make a sound start on the road to reading and writing;

- a high degree of attention to establishing good standards of behaviour reinforced by praise and under-pinned by such strategies as stories depicting human relationships and values;

- the assessment of the children's progress and attainment as an integral part of the programme of work. Much of this is achieved by the close observation of children's responses but some schools also used diagnostic tests successfully;

- meeting the demands of combining a prolonged reception period, caused by early entry, with those of the National Curriculum as pupils reach statutory age.

43.   In sum, the findings of this survey show that establishing high-quality provision for children in the reception class is a very worthwhile investment, particularly in areas where nursery or other forms of pre-school provision are sparse. The strong indication that primary schools are steadily improving the work of reception classes promises well for the future.